DISORDERLY CONDUCT

DISORDERLY CONDUCT

CONDUCT

Real-life comedy from the courtrooms

RODNEY JONES, CHARLES SEVILLA & GERALD UELMEN

Illustrated by Lee Lorenz

ANGUS
& ROBERTSON
PUBLISHERS

To the lawyers who work in the pits,
and manage to keep their sense of humour

ANGUS & ROBERTSON PUBLISHERS

16 Golden Square, London W1R 4BN,
United Kingdom

First published in the United Kingdom by
Angus & Robertson (UK) in 1988

Copyright © 1987 by Rodney R. Jones, Charles M. Sevilla, Gerald F. Uelmen
Illustrations copyright © 1987 by Lee Lorenz

Printed in Great Britain by Richard Clay Ltd, Bungay, Suffolk

British Library Cataloguing in Publication Data
Disorderly conduct : real life comedy from
   the courtrooms.
   1. United States. Law courts
   I. Jones, Ridney R. II. Sevilla, Charles M.
   III. Uelmen, Gerald F.
   347.307'1

ISBN 0 207 16000 7

CONTENTS

FOREWORD

Each of the vignettes appearing in this book actually took place in a courtroom. While the vast majority occurred in courtrooms of the United States, we have occasionally reached across the border to Canada, or even across the ocean to England. While the drama which takes place in courtrooms is frequently portrayed by the media, the humor is too often overlooked. It is all preserved, however, in the verbatim transcripts taken down by Court Reporter. Those were our primary source.

Many of the selections have appeared in a bimonthly column by Charles M. Sevilla, called "Great Moments in Courtroom History," published in both the *Forum* of California Attorneys for Criminal Justice and the *Champion* of the National Association of Criminal Defense Lawyers. We have also drawn on the collection of Judge William B. Burleigh of the Monterey, California Municipal Court, and the occasional excerpts published in *Dicta*, the magazine of the San Diego Bar Association. Permission is gratefully acknowledged.

Rodney R. Jones
Charles M. Sevilla
Gerald F. Uelmen

1

JUDICIAL
TEMPERAMENT

"The acme of judicial distinction means the ability to look a lawyer straight in the eyes for two hours and not hear a damn word he says."
CHIEF JUSTICE JOHN MARSHALL

"Impartial, adj: Unable to perceive any promise of personal advantage from espousing either side of a controversy or adopting either of two conflicting opinions."

AMBROSE BIERCE

"If I had me a job to pick out, I'd be a judge. I've looked over all th' others and that's th' on'y wan that suits. I have th' judicyal timperamint. I hate wurruk."
MR. DOOLEY (FINLEY PETER DUNNE)

THE COURT	I am very careful in these cases.
COUNSEL	I understand.
THE COURT	I am more careful in these cases than any other. The jury gets the case purely from the evidence. I can be so impeccably fair.
COUNSEL	I never questioned your fairness. I beg the indulgence of the court.
THE COURT	This is something you have to be born with, a gift.
COUNSEL	I concede this.
THE COURT	I have that gift. It is a tremendous gift and not many judges have the tremendous gift of fairness. It is something that I have to admit, and I admit it with a great deal of pride, but with a great deal of humility. I have it. I have an information, so to speak. It is what has made me a good student in constitutional law. I suppose so. It is what made it possible for me to perhaps pass the bar examination without an error in the entire examination that I went through.

I have that gift of fairness. I also have a gift of comprehensive thinking. I think all the way around every subject and get its interrelated parts and put them together as I go piece by piece, step by step. I have this, and I almost have the gift of reading minds and the thoughts of the individual.

. . . .

THE COURT	A curse on you, Kittle [the prosecutor] and a curse on your house and the whole damned Federal Crown for setting these cases down on Friday. I've told you about this before. Get a transcript with my profanity, Kittle, and give it to whoever is in charge there.
PROSECUTOR	Your Honor, this matter was set down by appearance not by—
THE COURT	I know, Kittle. You don't send out the instructions. Just a minute. I'll deal with it right now. Give me the information and if you do that, which I suspect you won't, Kittle, tell them I had a scowl on my face.
PROSECUTOR	Very well, Your Honor.
THE COURT	All right, read the charge.
CLERK	Joseph Arthur M., you are charged that at the City of Vancouver, Province of British Columbia, on the 25th day of January, A.D. 1979 you did unlawfully possess a narcotic, to wit, cannabis (marijuana), contrary to the provisions of the Narcotic Control Act. How do you plead to this charge, guilty or not guilty?
DEFENDANT	Guilty.
THE COURT	Go ahead, Mr. Kittle, tell me the heinous circumstances surrounding this offense.
PROSECUTOR	At approximately 2:15 a.m., January 25, a search was being conducted of the accused's room. He was found lying on the bed awake and in between the mattresses was found one plastic baggie containing

11

five small plastic baggies containing suspected marijuana. A conversation ensued. "Do you know what this is?" Answer, "Yes." Question, "Is it Michelle's?" Answer, "No." And there was further conversation which I think is unnecessary in this respect.

THE COURT   Any record?

PROSECUTOR   I have none, Your Honor.

THE COURT   How old are you, M?

DEFENDANT   Nineteen.

THE COURT   How long have you lived in Vancouver?

DEFENDANT   Off and on for the last two years.

THE COURT   Are you living with your parents or on your own?

DEFENDANT   On my own.

THE COURT   What do you do for a living?

DEFENDANT   I'm an insulator by trade on an apprenticeship.

THE COURT   You won't know why I'm doing this, M., because I think you're a useless idle bum who pretends to be a citizen of Canada and flagrantly breaks the law of Canada doing little or no good to yourself or your country. I have not much use for you or your type, a bunch of long-haired freaks, and you won't understand why I'm giving you an absolute discharge, but I'm doing it because I'm vexed with the Crown. An absolute discharge. Get out. No one will ever know how lucky you are. You certainly won't. You haven't got the brains. Tell them that too, would you, Kittle, and tell them that's the Friday routine from here on in.

PROSECUTOR   Yes, Your Honor.

. . . .

COUNSEL   I want the record also to reflect that the court has made noises on the record indicating a "tsk" sort of sound, so that the record can at least show . . .

THE COURT   For the record, it is spelled t-s-k, I think. Well, Counsel, I would like the record to reflect that your attitude is petulant, childlike and totally and thoroughly unprofessional.

COUNSEL   I respectfully disagree with the court.

THE COURT   Well, you have your right to disagree, but we have disagreed before and I certainly disagree with you now. The record is probably as long as you are tall already about statements that have been made by you.

COUNSEL   The record should reflect that I'm short, Your Honor.

THE COURT   Well, the record may also reflect that my patience with you has about reached the point of your height as well.

. . . .

THE COURT   [to defense attorney]: The court suggests to you that the questioning of this witness

13

has been exhausted. You have three more minutes. No more.

COUNSEL I am sorry, Your Honor. I am sorry I have irritated you.

THE COURT You are not irritating me at all, sir. You have a perfect right to make a record.

COUNSEL Your Honor, you yelled—you have yelled at me twice within the last two minutes. You are scowling at me now. You tell me I only have three minutes left and then you tell me I am not irritating you. Your Honor, I am sorry, but I can't help when you yell at me but feel that I have irritated you.

THE COURT I am not yelling at you at all.

COUNSEL Not at this moment you are not, Your Honor, but you have yelled at me twice in the last two minutes.

THE COURT Well, I don't agree with you that I have yelled at you.

COUNSEL You are pointing your fingers at me, Your Honor.

THE COURT Just a moment.

COUNSEL You are pointing your fingers at me, sir.

THE COURT I am not.

COUNSEL You are pointing two fingers at me this very minute, Your Honor. Would you please not point at me like that? You are still pointing.

THE COURT Counsel, Counsel.

COUNSEL Yes, Your Honor.

THE COURT Please remember that you are addressing a Superior Court Judge and behave yourself.

14

Counsel	I am.
The court	Now, I am making my ruling and I said you only have three more minutes. That's all you have. Is that clear? Now, if you interpret that as shouting you may do so. Now please proceed.
Counsel	Your Honor, I wonder if we might have a recess. Frankly, Your Honor, I am upset. May we have a recess for a few minutes?
The court	Well, that's a reasonable request. How long a recess do you want?
Counsel	Oh, I think ten minutes would be enough.
The court	Sir?
Counsel	Ten minutes.
The court	Ten minute recess.

. . . .

Counsel	In this case, my defense disputes the · seriousness of the injury; no medical attention, no sutures, no loss of consciousness, nothing. In fact, when I last saw the young gentleman, the remnant was a black eye, which I don't think comes under the purview of serious injury.
D.A.	Yeah.
The court	Mr. Prosecutor?
D.A.	Just observing. I wonder how it feels to get punched in the mouth. I wonder if that's a 242 or 245.
The court	You may find out if you keep on interrupting.

"I'd give it another five minutes, Your Honor. The
tension's beginning to mount."

. . . .

COUNSEL Judge, may I be heard on the matter of
bond on appeal and possible stay of
execution of the sentence?

THE COURT Yes. Denied.

. . . .

D.A. Is Your Honor saying that the magistrate
should have gone into the 100
investigations that the officer talks about at
page 413? Is that what you're saying?

THE COURT I've just read 800 pages of your argument
and questions, and let me instruct you, let
me direct you that I do not like and will
not accept the Socratic form of argument.

D.A. All right.

THE COURT Do not ask the Court a question again.

D.A. All right. Is Your Honor saying . . .

. . . .

THE COURT The amount of fees being asked for—what
does this mean, "Multiplied by three,"
Mr. W.?

COUNSEL Your Honor, there is authority for a
multiplication factor based upon the
difficulty of the case.

THE COURT Can you tell me what was difficult about
this case?

COUNSEL Well, Your Honor, basically dealing with

17

	Your Honor is what was difficult about the case.
THE COURT	What was that again? I didn't hear.
COUNSEL	I said dealing with Your Honor was what was difficult.
THE COURT	Mr. W., you know I find you particularly offensive and I want you to know.
COUNSEL	Your Honor—
THE COURT	Now just a minute. Don't you come in to this courtroom and make a remark like that.
COUNSEL	Your Honor asked me the question.
THE COURT	I have stood you enough in this courtroom. This petition is denied. The Government doesn't have to answer it.
COUNSEL	Very well, Your Honor. I also ask you to expunge some remarks that you made gratuitously in an order.
THE COURT	That motion is denied.
COUNSEL	And Your Honor continues to make gratuitous remarks and continues to—
THE COURT	That motion is denied.
COUNSEL	Thank you very much, Your Honor.

. . . .

THE COURT	Sir, I have no intention of waiting for courts of appeal. They are no longer courts. They are nothing except snags for time. Period.
COUNSEL	Well, I'm not indicating that we should.
THE COURT	I have long since given up; long, long

since given up. As far as I'm concerned the appellate situation in this state is a horror. It makes the trial situation equally poor. And if we sit around waiting for those people to take a laxative, it's the slowest working laxative in the world. I have been given a responsibility and by God I'm going to carry it out. And the blessed Supreme Court can sit up there as long as it wants and die of old age. I'm not going to wait on them to say anything anymore. I've waited and waited and waited for twenty years. Forget it.

. . . .

COUNSEL   Shot down again.
THE COURT   Any other foundations upon which you would like to urge the admissibility of this?
COUNSEL   It's going to take your overruling my—
THE COURT   That's fine. I am pleased to do it.
COUNSEL   I don't want you to be pleased to do it. I would like for you to say it's a very close question.
THE COURT   This is an extremely close question. But having delicately balanced the points of law in favor and the points of law opposed, I am obligated, in following the mandates of the Evidence Code and the higher courts, despite any personal feelings I may have to the contrary, because my duty here is not to impose my personal feelings on my rulings, but to follow the

19

law. And this is one of those occasions where I am discharging my duties solely and simply. And I wouldn't admit this Goddamn thing if you paid me.

. . . .

D.A.   Did you say that to the investigating officer?

WITNESS   Didn't I tell you I couldn't remember back that far?

D.A.   So, you don't remember saying that? Is that what you are telling me? You don't remember?

WITNESS   I know what I just told you. Do you?

THE COURT   Did you say that to the officer?

WITNESS   What did I just say?

THE COURT   I'm asking you to answer my question.

WITNESS   I just told you if I can't remember back that far how in the hell am I going to answer it?

THE COURT   Lucky you are inside, I can see that.

WITNESS   Yeah, stupid, they made you a judge, didn't they?

THE COURT   Yes, that is right, but I am on the outside.

WITNESS   That is all right, asshole. I will be out there soon.

. . . .

THE COURT   I would like to cite you for contempt of court—don't say anything until I finish—

20

every time you say something I will cite you for contempt.

I ruled on your motion and then you pointed a finger at the court in the immediate view and presence of the court, and you were waving your arms and fingering at me and shouting.

Next count, when both counsel were coming into my chambers yesterday to discuss the jury instructions you were laughing and talking loud as you came into chambers completely ignoring my presence in my own chambers. For a whole minute you were not even facing me. You were talking to Mr. K. and telling him some story with loud laughter.

Today at 9:15 A.M., your chair was positioned sideways 40 degrees tilted. You were facing the jurors, not the court when I came in.

Next count, you were playing fingers on the counsel table like playing piano so loud that it disturbed the court, and I observed the court reporter looking at your face.

In the morning when I came into the courtroom at 9:00 I said "Good morning" to you and to the prosecutor. You, as usual for the past five days, you didn't even look at me. You were whistling.

Now, to these counts what do you have —would you like to explain something away before I decide what to do with you?

COUNSEL   You catch me completely—

THE COURT	Are you apologizing?
COUNSEL	If you were offended, absolutely. I would apologize.
THE COURT	Okay. Counsel, I have a son who is about your age. You are very intelligent. Your future is so bright. You are a tremendously great lawyer.
	I have been in your position as defense lawyer. Until just yesterday I was sitting right there. I love you. You as a great lawyer must change your attitude, my goodness sake, for your own bright future. You are just—you said eight years. It is just a beginning. You have a bright future ahead of you. Don't screw up, please.
	Case dismissed.

. . . .

WITNESS	(prison inmate): I'm not bragging or anything, but I want you to know I've got a law degree from LaSalle and I'm just telling you that so you'll know you're not dealing with a dummy.
THE COURT	I'd like you to know I have a law degree from the University of Washington, and you're not dealing with one either.

. . . .

COUNSEL	Your honor . . .
THE COURT	Don't interrupt.
COUNSEL	But, Your Honor . . .

THE COURT Don't speak until after I arraign your client.

Sir, you are charged in a four-count indictment with the offenses of assault with a deadly weapon, robbery, mayhem, and receiving stolen property. How do you plead?

COUNSEL My client doesn't understand English.

. . . .

COUNSEL Your Honor, I don't mean to be facetious. In all seriousness, this is a case that literally cries out for justice.

THE COURT Counselor, everyone receives justice in this court.

COUNSEL Yes, Your Honor, but this case cries out for additional justice.

THE COURT I'm sorry counselor; we're all out of additional justice. We used it up on the morning calendar.

. . . .

THE COURT Do you know what Carl Sandburg said?

COUNSEL "The fog comes in under the cat's feet?"

THE COURT But he said more cogently, "In the hangman's house we stay off some subjects."

COUNSEL I see.

THE COURT Yes.

2

THE PLEADINGS

"In law, it is good policy to never plead what you need not, lest you oblige yourself to prove what you can not."

ABRAHAM LINCOLN

"It is a maxim among these lawyers, that whatever hath been done before, may legally be done again: and therefore they take special care to record all the decisions formerly made against common justice, and the general reason of mankind. These, under the name of precedents, they produce as authorities, to justify the most iniquitous opinions; and the judges never fail of directing accordingly."

JONATHAN SWIFT

The penalty the learned Lord Chancellor,
Thomas Egerton (1603–1617), imposed on
attorney Richard Mylward for drawing a
replication containing 120 pages when, in
the Chancellor's opinion, 16 would have
sufficed:

"It is therefore ordered that the warden
of the Fleet shall take the said Richard
Mylward . . . into his custody, and shall
bring him unto Westminster Hall on
Saturday next . . . and there and then
shall cut a hole in the myddest of the
same engrossed replication . . . and put
the said Richard's head through the same
hole, and so let the same replication hang
about his shoulders with the written side
outward; and then, the same so hanging,
shall lead the same Richard, bare headed
and bare faced, round Westminster Hall,
whilst the courts are sitting, and shall shew
him at the bar of every of the three courts
within the Hall."

. . . .

A Florida State Prison inmate filed a
civil rights suit over allegedly unsanitary
prison conditions. He sent the local federal
court a plastic envelope containing several
dead roaches as evidence of roach
infestation. Assuming it was an isolated
incident, court officials thought little of
the gesture.

Several months later, the prisoner filed a motion for summary judgment and included a separate note that stated, "Dear Mr. Clerk: Please Find enclosed, one (1) mouse and mark as Exhibit M . . . and a motion to the honorable judge."

Court employees dutifully removed the dead rodent from its plastic coffin, placed it in a jar of formaldehyde and filed it with the clerk to preserve the chain of evidence.

But things really got out of hand when the prisoner filed a motion for acceptance for further evidence, and included a less carefully preserved mouse. This exhibit was "a little riper" than the previous specimens, according to court staff.

The judge put an end to the affair ordering the prisoner to content himself with sending written descriptions of such physical evidence.

In addition to probably violating U.S. postal regulations, the judge pointed out, any further such evidence would prompt him to dismiss the case.

. . . .

The following answers to interrogatories were filed by the wife in a divorce action:

52. Do you have a proposal to settle this case amicably?

Answer: Yes.

53. Assuming your answer to the preceding interrogatory is in the affirmative, please state such proposal.

Answer: Use a silver bullet or a wooden stake as is appropriate in these cases.

In Juvenile Court a complaint was filed against a mother under the Welfare and Institutions Code for encouraging a minor to live an immortal life.

Criminal Complaint:

For a further and separate cause of complaint being a different offense from but connected in its commission with the charge(s) set forth in the preceding count(s) hereof, complainant further complainsand says: That said defendant(s), on or about the 17th day of November, 1984, at the County of Monterey, State of California, did commit the crime of VIOLATION of MONTEREY COUNTY ORDINANCE SECTION 11.88.020 a MISDEMEANOR, committed as follows, to-wit: That at said time and place the said defendant(s) did willfully and unlawfully shoot and discharge a fireman within a portion of the unincorporated territory of the County of

Monterey where such shooting and discharging is prohibited.

· · · · · · · · · · · · · · · ·

The primary issue presented on this appeal regards the legal adequacy of the indictment under which Henderson has been tried, convicted and sentenced. That indictment, in pertinent part, reads as follows:

> The Grand Jurors for the State of Mississippi, . . . upon their oaths present: That Jacob Henderson . . . on the 15th day of May, A.D., 1982.
> The store building there situated, the property of Metro Auto Painting, Inc., . . . in which store building was kept for sale or use valuable things, to-wit: goods, ware and merchandise unlawfully, feloniously and burglariously did break and enter, with intent the goods, wares and merchandise of said Metro Auto Painting then and there being in said store building unlawfully, feloniously and then and there being in said store building burglariously to take, steal and carry away; And . . . the property of the said Metro Auto Painting then and there being in said store building did then and there unlawfully, feloniously and burglariously take, steal and carry away the aforesaid property, he, the said Jacob Henderson, having been twice previously convicted of felonies, to-wit: . . .

"Don't drop it, pal. It's a subpoena."

The remainder of the indictment charges Henderson with being a recidivist.

Henderson, no doubt offended, demurred. In support, he presented an expert witness, Ann Dreher, who had been a teacher of English for nine years. Ms. Dreher testified that, when read consistent with accepted rules of English grammar, the indictment did not charge Jacob Henderson with doing anything; rather it charged that goods, ware and merchandise broke and entered the paint store. The trial judge overruled the objection and the motion, but not without reservation. He stated:

> [T]his same objection has been made numerous times. It is one of Mr. Hailey's pets. [B]ut as far as I know no one has elected to appeal and I'm going to follow the decision whether it is grammatically correct or not. I have repeatedly begged for six years or five years for the district attorney not to use this form. It is very poor English. It is impossible English. . . . In addition to being very poor English, it also charges him with the crime of larceny, which is not necessary to include in an indictment for burglary. I never did understand the reason for that. I again ask the district attorney not to use this form. It's archaic. Even Shakespeare could not understand the grammatical construction of this

31

indictment. But the objection will be overruled.

Answer to complaint for damages against railroad company:

The defendant further specially excepts to said petition where it is alleged that the plaintiff, upon discovering that the wooden stool was wet, raised the same and squatted with his feet poised on the porcelain bowl of the commode, from which roosting position he says his foot slipped causing him to fall to the great detriment of his left testicle, for the reason that it is obvious that the said commode with its full moon contours was rightfully and properly designed for the comfort of sitters only, being equipped with neither spurs, stirrups nor toeholds for boots or shoes: this defendant, therefore, was not legally required to foresee that the plaintiff, traveling on its modern, air-conditioned deluxe passenger train would so persist in his barnyard predilections as to trample upon its elegant toilet fixture in the barbaric style of horse and buggy days.

For further answer, if needed, this defendant enters its general denial and specially pleads that the plaintiff should not be allowed to recover any sum against it for the reason that the plaintiff

is, in truth and in fact, a chronic
squatter, born and bred to the custom of
the corn crib, and, although a com-
paratively young man, is unable to adapt
himself to the cultural refinements of a
New Deal civilization, and should have,
therefore, in the exercise of due care
deferred taking the Crazy Water Crystals
until such time when he could be at
home secure and sure-footed on his own
dung-hill or with his feet planted solidly
on the flat boards of his own old
fashioned two-holer.

3

POLICE
INVESTIGATION

"The criminal is to go free because the constable has blundered."
                    JUSTICE BENJAMIN N. CARDOZO

"A policeman's lot is not a happy one."
                    ARTHUR S. GILBERT

Federal Court of Appeals opinion:

The agents involved speak an almost impenetrable jargon. They do not get into their cars; they enter official government vehicles. They do not get out of or leave their cars, they exit them. They do not go somewhere; they proceed. They do not go to a particular place; they proceed to its vicinity. They do not watch or look; they surveille. They never see anything; they observe it. No one tells them anything; they are advised. A person does not tell them his name; he identifies himself. A person does not say something; he indicates. They do not listen to a telephone conversation; they monitor it. People telephoning to each other do not say "hello"; they exchange greetings. An agent does not hand money to an informer to make a buy; he advances previously recorded official government funds. To an agent, a list of serial numbers does not list serial numbers, it depicts Federal Reserve Notes. An agent does not say what an exhibit is; he says that it purports to be. The agents preface answers to simple and direct questions with "to my knowledge." They cannot describe a conversation by saying "he said" and "I said"; they speak in conclusions. Sometimes it takes the combined efforts of counsel and the judge to get them to state who said what.

Under cross examination, they seem unable to give a direct answer to a question, they either spout conclusions or do not understand. This often gives the prosecutor, under the guise of an objection, an opportunity to suggest an answer, which is then obligingly given.

. . . .

Police report in a rape case: "The defendant, when first observed, was atop the victim in a sublime position."

. . . .

COUNSEL Would you observe these photographs and tell me if these items were seen by you that day?

POLICE OFFICER Yes, sir, all items depicted in the five photos were later observed by this officer while I was observing the said property which was observed in the trunk of the vehicle.

. . . .

Police report description of arrest:
Defendant was confronted and he again failed to stop and when the officer attempted to stop him by the use of a baton around his neck, defendant freed himself and began moving toward the officer in a threatening manner. The officer struck defendant on the head with

37

his baton. It was then observed that defendant appeared to be glassy eyed and had a distant stare commonly associated with people under the influence of PCP.

. . . .

COUNSEL	And then after you saw Mr. G, you came up to him—identified yourself?
POLICE OFFICER	Yes, sir.
COUNSEL	Told him in English, probably then in Spanish, that he was under arrest?
POLICE OFFICER	Yes, sir.
COUNSEL	Did you have your weapon drawn as you approached him, sir?
POLICE OFFICER	Indeed I did, sir.
COUNSEL	You told him at this time he was under arrest?
POLICE OFFICER	Yes, sir, I did.
COUNSEL	Mr. G, by the way, was complying with your orders?
POLICE OFFICER	Indeed he was.
COUNSEL	Made no resistance?
POLICE OFFICER	No, sir, he did not.
COUNSEL	Cooperated with you in every way?
POLICE OFFICER	Very cooperative.
COUNSEL	And you had your gun out during this entire period?
POLICE OFFICER	That is correct, sir.
COUNSEL	Where was the gun pointed, sir—at his stomach, midsection, head?
POLICE OFFICER	It was nestled right down the back of his neck.

COUNSEL — Did you say anything to Mr. G, by the way, sir, concerning what would happen if he tried to move or get away?

POLICE OFFICER — I said I would try to blow his head off.

COUNSEL — It was during this time, when Mr. G had that .38 special cradled on the back of his neck, that you told him his rights under Miranda. Is that correct?

POLICE OFFICER — Yes, sir.

. . . .

COUNSEL — Can you tell us what you did with regard to the pat search of Mr. L?

POLICE OFFICER — I began a grasping search of the clothing. And I searched him from the top down until I got to his pants in the groin area and then I felt a hard object.

COUNSEL — And what occurred when you felt that hard object?

POLICE OFFICER — I grabbed at it. I felt the hard object. I grabbed it a little bit closer to try to get the outline of what it was, when L said, "It's my dick."

COUNSEL — And then what happened?

POLICE OFFICER — He said, "I'll get it."

COUNSEL — Officer, you were frightened by what occurred out there; is that right?

POLICE OFFICER — Yes.

COUNSEL — Well what, if anything, had Mr. L done to you that caused you to be frightened? Did telling you you were feeling his dick, did that frighten you?

"I must warn you that anything you say may be taken
down and used against you."

POLICE OFFICER No.

COUNSEL Did he do anything at all that caused you
to be frightened by anything he did or
said?

POLICE OFFICER It became a concern to me when I felt
the hard object in his pants, first of all.
Then when I continued to feel it and he
said, "It's my dick," I got a little more
concerned, you know, when he reached in
his pants to get that hard object, which I
had almost positively identified as a gun.

· · · · · · · · · · · · · · · ·

COUNSEL Where was she?

POLICE OFFICER In the living room.

COUNSEL Is that where you placed her under arrest
also?

POLICE OFFICER Yes.

COUNSEL Did you then unarrest the defendant?

POLICE OFFICER Yes.

COUNSEL How did you communicate that to her?

POLICE OFFICER I told her she wasn't under arrest no more.

COUNSEL And then did you arrest her again?

POLICE OFFICER Yes.

COUNSEL And then did you unarrest her again?

POLICE OFFICER Yes.

COUNSEL When did the second unarrest take place?

POLICE OFFICER When the captain told me I was going to
be reprimanded.

COUNSEL For arresting her or unarresting her?

POLICE OFFICER No, arresting her.

COUNSEL   So you arrested the lady, the captain told you to unarrest her, and the captain told you you would be reprimanded for arresting her, then you arrested her again?

POLICE OFFICER   I arrested her, the captain told me to unarrest her, and knowing that the captain was wrong I arrested her again and then he told me, well you'd better unarrest her. And I unarrested her.

. . . .

D.A.   Then what did you do?
POLICE OFFICER   I began kicking in the door.
D.A.   Were you wearing boots?
POLICE OFFICER   Yes, sir, size 12.
D.A.   How many times did you kick the door?
POLICE OFFICER   About ten.
D.A.   What was Sergeant Harp doing while you were kicking the door?
POLICE OFFICER   Laughing at me.

. . . .

Two police officers extracted a confession from a suspect by advising him the Xerox machine was a lie detector. First they put a colander—a salad strainer —over the suspect's head and wired it to the duplicating machine. Then, under the Xerox lid they placed a slip of paper reading "He Is Lying!" Every time the

42

suspect answered a question, an officer
would press the duplicating button and out
would pop a Xeroxed "He Is Lying!"
Finally shaken, the suspect told all. His
confession was thrown out by a judge who
was not amused.

4

ACCIDENT REPORTS

"It shall be a vexation only to understand the report."
                                        ISAIAH, 28:19

"The reports of my death are greatly exaggerated."
                                        MARK TWAIN

Coming home, I drove into the wrong house and collided with a tree I don't have.

. . . .

The other car collided with mine without giving warning of its intentions.

. . . .

I thought my window was down, but found it was up when I put my hand through it.

. . . .

I collided with a stationary truck coming the other way.

. . . .

A truck backed through my windshield into my wife's face.

. . . .

A pedestrian hit me and went under my car.

. . . .

The guy was all over the road. I had to swerve a number of times before I hit him.

. . . .

I pulled away from the side of the road, glanced at my mother-in-law, and headed over the embankment.

. . . .

In my attempt to kill a fly, I drove into a telephone pole.

. . . .

I had been shopping for plants all day, and was on my way home. As I reached an intersection, a hedge sprang up obscuring my vision. I did not see the other car.

. . . .

I had been driving my car for forty years when I fell asleep at the wheel and had an accident.

. . . .

I was on my way to the doctor's with rear end trouble when my universal joint gave way causing me to have an accident.

. . . .

As I approached the intersection, a stop sign appeared in a place where no stop sign had ever appeared before. I was unable to stop in time to avoid the accident.

. . . .

To avoid hitting the bumper of the car in front, I struck the pedestrian.

. . . .

My car was legally parked as it backed into the other vehicle.

. . . .

An invisible car came out of nowhere, struck my vehicle and vanished.

. . . .

I told the police that I was not injured but on removing my hat, I found that I had a skull fracture.

. . . .

I was sure the old fellow would never make it to the other side of the roadway when I struck him.

. . . .

The pedestrian had no idea which direction to go, so I ran over him.

. . . .

I saw the slow moving, sad-faced gentleman as he bounced off my car.

. . . .

The indirect cause of this accident was a little guy in a small car with a big mouth.

. . . .

I was thrown from my car as it left the road. I was later found in a ditch by some stray cows.

. . . .

The telephone pole was approaching fast. I was attempting to swerve out of its path when it struck my front end.

. . . .

I was unable to stop in time, and my car crashed into the other vehicle. The driver and passengers then left immediately for a vacation with injuries.

. . . .

I was struck by a beer bottle in the rear head.

. . . .

After approximately two or three seconds I felt a numbness which came to my right rear buttock.

5

THE ADVOCATES

"The trial lawyer does what Socrates was executed for: making the worse argument appear the stronger."

JUDGE IRVING KAUFMAN

"Then, if at any time you find you have the worst end of the staff, leave off your cause and fall upon the person of your adversary."

JOHN WILSON

"It isn't the bad lawyers who are screwing up the justice system in this country—it's the good lawyers. If you have two competent lawyers on opposite sides, a trial that should take three days could easily last six months."

ART BUCHWALD

D.A.	Your Honor, prior to calling my first witness, I'd like to state for the record that immediately prior to starting this proceeding and in open court while His Honor was in chambers, defense counsel called me a punk three times and called me a shit once. I don't know what explanation he has for that, but I wanted to put it on the record before we started this. It had to do with this proceeding.

. . . .

D.A.	This matter is here for trial today.
THE COURT	People ready?
D.A.	Yes, but we move to dismiss in the interest of justice.
THE COURT	What is the interest of justice?
D.A.	The case sucks.

. . . .

COUNSEL	That's bullshit. We spent 45 minutes.
THE COURT	You mustn't use bad language because the appellate court doesn't like that. You can say it's nonsense.
COUNSEL	It's nonsense, Your Honor.
THE COURT	That is not a legal objection.

. . . .

COUNSEL	My sole purpose in this little monologue is to record that understanding on the

record, and if there is any disagreement with my understanding by counsel for the defendants, which I believe there is not, to ask that that be recorded so that there be no misunderstanding subsequently by any party to this case or any third parties as to what we intend to provide.

THE COURT My problem with what you have said is simply that I am not altogether sure that I understand what you have said.

. . . .

SE ATTORNEY Then I object to the District Attorney objecting to my objecting to standard legal objections.

. . . .

COUNSEL The D.A. stated that he invited me to discuss these matters with him but so far he has demurred. I think the record should reflect he challenged me to a fight this morning out in the hallway, to go outside and man to man, one to one. I think that's all I need to say.

D.A. Counsel flatters himself. Even in my most frivolous moments I would not consider challenging him to any sort of a fight. I would challenge him to something in the nature of a debate where he might have to look me in the eye and say some of these

things that he has said on this document
which he snuck under the door this
morning. Beyond that, he's a pantywaist.

. . . .

DEFENDANT	Judge, I want you to appoint me another lawyer.
THE COURT	And why is that?
DEFENDANT	Because the P.D. isn't interested in my case.
THE COURT	(to public defender) Do you have any comments on defendant's motion?
PUBLIC DEFENDER	I'm sorry, Your Honor, I wasn't listening.

. . . .

COUNSEL	Your Honor, I have just three or four questions.
THE COURT	Oh, come on, Counsel. How can you possibly think of another question?
COUNSEL	Well, I had a few minutes, and I was able to.
THE COURT	That's enough.
COUNSEL	Your Honor, for the record, I do believe I have a right to recross after co-counsel has crossed. It's only three or four questions.
THE COURT	I don't give a damn if you have a right. The question is, do you have the sense not to?
COUNSEL	Obviously not. I made the request.
THE COURT	Ask your question.

"If it please the Court, may I point out that I requested to approach the Bench before learned counsel requested to approach the Bench."

. . . .

The defendant was charged with murder. After arraignment, the matter of setting bail became a heated issue. The People urged that $50,000 should be the minimum amount because the defendant had a long record.

The deputy public defender was momentarily stunned at the large bail demand, but he regained his composure and said, "That amount of bail is outrageously excessive . . . er well, after all, this is only the defendant's first murder."

. . . .

"Today we conclude that when an attorney for a criminal defendant sleeps through a substantial portion of the trial, such conduct is inherently prejudicial and thus no separate showing of prejudice is necessary. Prejudice is inherent in this case because unconscious or sleeping counsel is equivalent to no counsel at all."

6
PICKING A JURY

"A jury consists of twelve persons of average ignorance."
                                                MARK TWAIN

"The man who wants a jury has a bad case."
        JUSTICE OLIVER WENDELL HOLMES, JR.

"A jury consists of 12 persons chosen to decide who has the better lawyer."

                                                ROBERT FROST

THE COURT	Do any of you prospective jurors know me?
JUROR	Yes.
THE COURT	I am pleased to see that I have—is our acquaintanceship close enough that you feel that it might be some impediment sitting as a juror?
JUROR	Yes, I feel it would. It's unfavorable.
THE COURT	It is unfavorable? Let's go to some of the other questions. You have never had any negative experience with law enforcement except perhaps sitting as a juror in my department; is that correct?
JUROR	No, it wasn't as a juror.
THE COURT	It was not?
JUROR	No.
THE COURT	Was it as a witness?
JUROR	You were the judge in a case that my husband was—you denied him a hearing for reinstatement to a job with the county.
THE COURT	I see.
JUROR	Twice, in fact.
THE COURT	You didn't testify in the matter?
JUROR	No, I did not.
THE COURT	So that your displeasure with me is merely the result of what I did in the case in which your husband was involved?
JUROR	Right.
THE COURT	All right. The loser is always displeased, I find.
JUROR	I have to live with the loser, though.
THE COURT	Touché. Well, I hope this experience will

be more pleasant for you if you are selected to serve as a juror.

JUROR   We don't think very highly of lawyers either, as a matter of fact.

THE COURT   Okay. When you heard about this case, did you form any opinion about the defendant's guilt or innocence?

JUROR   Not really. I just assumed that he had committed the crime.

. . . .

COUNSEL   Have any of the prospective jurors ever been victims of a crime?

JUROR   Well, I'm not sure if this is considered a victim, but a couple weeks—no, a couple of months ago I was mowing my lawn and there was a guy on my lawn in the nude. That's about the only thing.

COUNSEL   Did you report that to the police?

JUROR   Yes.

COUNSEL   Did they come on to your place then?

JUROR   Yes, right away. It was three officers that came over.

COUNSEL   Did they catch the guy?

JUROR   I don't know. I don't think so.

COUNSEL   Did you give them a description, et cetera, telling the officers what he was doing?

JUROR   Well, I told them what I had seen, but he was a real tall person, so I just saw from the waist down.

. . . .

COUNSEL   Can you participate in an endeavor in
          which the ultimate result might be death
          by lethal injection?
JUROR   They do that up in Huntsville, don't they?
          Yeah, I guess I could do it if it was on a
          weekend.
COUNSEL   And [next juror] you, sir?
JUROR   Yes, I think it's too quick.
COUNSEL   And you, sir?
JUROR   It should be left up to the victims' families
          rather than the courts.
COUNSEL   You know that my client is charged with
          robbing a Seven-Eleven, tying up two
          employees and shooting them both in the
          head as he fled. Now if the state offers
          you evidence to prove these facts, would
          you—
JUROR   He's gone!

. . . .

THE COURT   Were you ever in the service?
JUROR   Yes, the Navy.
THE COURT   How long?
JUROR   29 days.
THE COURT   Without going into detail, why were you
            discharged?
JUROR   They found out I was allergic to wool and
            salt water.

62

. . . .

THE COURT	You feel one side or the other is not starting even here?
JUROR	Yes, sir.
THE COURT	Is there some particular question that you heard that triggered that?
JUROR	No, sir. May I be candid with you?
THE COURT	Yes.
JUROR	Okay. My daughter is Susan, who was just excused by the D.A.
THE COURT	I understand.
JUROR	And without being held liable, my personal feelings, I feel the D.A. is a jerk.
THE COURT	I think I know enough, Mr. G. It is not necessary to state anything more. You may be excused.

. . . .

Voir dire in a drunk driving case:

COUNSEL	Do you think that before the People can prove their case to you, or to all of you beyond a reasonable doubt, that that proof must include scientific evidence that the defendant had blood in his alcohol?

. . . .

COUNSEL	Ladies of the jury, the next couple of questions I have to ask you, you may consider them personal in nature. I ask

"Are we to understand, then, that you would have no
scruples about imposing the death penalty?"

you please do not consider me to be invading your privacy in any way. Do the concepts of rape and/or sodomy leave you with such a bad taste in your mouth?

. . . .

COUNSEL If the law or the instructions conflict with your beliefs, will you still accept the law without question?

JUROR Well, that is what I want to make clear. I don't know what those beliefs are; that is what I have tried to understand. And so I'm finding it difficult to answer that question given those terms used.

COUNSEL Can you tell us that you would follow the court's instructions regardless of what else happened for you during the course of the trial?

JUROR Cognitively, yes. Rationally, yes. Emotionally, effectively, I don't know. Or perhaps effectively, yes, and rationally, no.

. . . .

COUNSEL Did you retain an attorney to represent you in those matters?

JUROR Yes, I did.

COUNSEL Were you satisfied with the services of the attorney or attorneys you had?

JUROR No, I was not.

COUNSEL Would that carry over to me or to any of the other attorneys?

JUROR Yes, it would.

COUNSEL Could you tell me briefly how it would carry over?

JUROR My opinion of attorneys, that they are one step lower than child molesters.

. . . .

COUNSEL How do you feel about criminal defense attorneys?

JUROR I think they should all be drowned at birth.

COUNSEL Well then, you are obviously biased for the prosecution?

JUROR What makes you think that, I hate prosecutors too.

. . . .

THE COURT Is there any reason you could not serve as a juror in this case?

JUROR I don't want to be away from my job that long.

THE COURT Can't they do without you at work?

JUROR Yes, but I don't want them to know it.

. . . .

COUNSEL Is there anything about your physical condition that might make it difficult for you to serve in this case?

JUROR No.

COUNSEL You don't have doctor appointments today
or the next couple of days?
JUROR No.
COUNSEL Do you have any physical problems with
your pregnancy?
JUROR I'm not pregnant.

7

THE DEFENDANT

"If there is any truth to the old proverb that 'one who is his own lawyer has a fool for a client,' the Court . . . bestows a constitutional right on the one to make a fool of himself."

JUSTICE HARRY BLACKMUN

"Litigant: A person about to give up his skin for the hope of retaining his bones."

AMBROSE BIERCE

"Most lawyers who win a case advise their clients that 'we have won.' And when justice has frowned upon their cause that 'you have lost.' "

LOUIS NIZER

DEFENDANT	I feel that I am being handicapped when the original recess was for me to find things throughout the transcript. I am taken back there. I can't even have a pencil. What possible defense can I have to make notes? Am I to carry a thought in my mind?
THE COURT	The pencil problem is an awful problem. The sheriff has a rule that no pencils are allowed, and not even felt pens, and so I have got no control over that.
DEFENDANT	The District Attorney has a pen and pencil and everything else. This is not equal defense.
THE COURT	The sheriffs have that rule, and it is a good rule. I am sure you understand the reason for it. On the one hand, I expect letting you have a pencil and felt tip pen would be no problem. But suppose somebody in here gets it away from you? That could be a very deadly weapon. You see?
DEFENDANT	I can understand that point.
THE COURT	How about a crayon? Can't you give him a crayon?
BAILIFF	I will check, Your Honor.
THE COURT	There is no prohibition on crayon, is there? You can sharpen it up a little bit. I can't make an order that you can have a pencil. I think I will make an order that you can have a crayon, and let's see if the sheriff's department gets that okay.

DEFENDANT	Yes, sir.
BAILIFF	I will try to find one, Your Honor.
THE COURT	Well, I have got some around here.

. . . .

Judge to a defendant: You have a right to a trial by jury, but you may waive that right. Which do you wish to do?

The defendant hesitated. His lawyer said firmly, "Waive." The defendant raised his hand and waved at the judge.

. . . .

THE COURT	You have to say, "I want it," and "I'm willing to give up my rights to have it come on earlier."
DEFENDANT	What rights?
THE COURT	It beats the hell out of me, ma'am. It says there in the Constitution.
DEFENDANT	I don't know what you're talking about, so I can't say.
THE COURT	In that event, we will continue right on as it is. Ma'am, I've got news for you. You've got this; now you're going to have to deal with it, and I don't intend to sit here and conduct a kindergarten playground.
DEFENDANT	I don't understand what you're saying: "Am I willing to give up my rights."
THE COURT	I don't give a good Goddamn whether you said it. All I'm saying is you have a right

to have it come on in 30 days. Now, what is it, ma'am? Is it something in the head there that doesn't click? Very good. We'll enter a plea of not guilty with a jury demand on your behalf. When do you want to go to trial, miss? You're a big girl.

DEFENDANT   I know it, Your Honor. I'm not accustomed to this.

THE COURT   I understand that you're not accustomed to it, but you don't also walk in here and just yence me around. I refuse to be so handled. I'm sorry. I do not intend to be so treated. I've got a number of things to do. I've got a number of people to handle. I've now set trial already for you.

DEFENDANT   Set it whenever you have to. If I'm here, I'm here. If I'm not, I'm not.

. . . .

THE COURT   The charge here is theft of frozen chickens. Are you the defendant, sir?

DEFENDANT   No, sir, I'm the guy who stole the chickens.

. . . .

THE COURT   Are you ready to proceed?

DEFENDANT   No, Your Honor, not at this time. Would you place my matter on second call or recall the case after the court takes a recession?

72

· · · · · · · · · · · · · · ·

COUNSEL   Now, you indicated that you were missing several items?
WITNESS   Yes.
COUNSEL   Cassettes?
WITNESS   Right.
COUNSEL   Do you recall the names of any of those cassettes?
WITNESS   Yes, but I couldn't name them all.
COUNSEL   What names do you recall?
WITNESS   Okay. *Rolling Stones Live,* it's a double album. Eddie Money, I can't think of the other ones.
DEFENDANT Pat Travis?
WITNESS   Right. Pat Travis.
COUNSEL   Shut up.
WITNESS   Two Pat Travis.

· · · · · · · · · · · · · · ·

DEFENDANT Can I ask her some questions?
THE COURT Just one moment.
DEFENDANT This bitch don't know me. She don't know who I am.
THE COURT Just one minute, sir. Please, when we direct our attention to human beings, we use different phraseology, okay?
DEFENDANT I don't give a fuck. This is my fucking life.
THE COURT You're going to give a fuck in this court, you hear me? You bug off.

"Most brilliantly argued self-representation I ever heard."

. . . .

DEFENDANT   Yes, Your Honor. I represented myself on
             a death penalty case in Santa Monica and
             I had one pro per on some attempted
             murder case here in L.A. and Norwalk and
             Long Beach and some armed robberies. I
             have been pro per for a few years, Your
             Honor.

THE COURT   What kind of success have you had in
             acting as your own lawyer?

DEFENDANT   I didn't get the death penalty, Your
             Honor.

. . . .

DEFENDANT   I would like to also be allowed movement
             in the courtroom.

THE COURT   You'd like what?

DEFENDANT   Movement in the courtroom without being
             followed by the Sheriff.

THE COURT   You can't do that.

DEFENDANT   I think it's inhibiting my defense. It's
             prejudicial to my defense.

THE COURT   It's up to you. You know, the courthouse,
             when I first practiced law here, had an
             iron cage for defendants who are
             incarcerated and they sat in the iron cage
             in the courtroom. Even though there is no
             cage, they still sit in what is a dock and
             obviously they're not allowed to wander
             around.

DEFENDANT   They used to feed Christians to lions.
That don't make it right.

. . . .

THE COURT   Each of you present as a defendant has
been charged with a public offense, and
this is the time set for your arraignment.
There will be no defecating or urinating
while I am giving the rights.

. . . .

THE COURT   You've been charged with armed robbery.
Do you want the court to appoint a lawyer
to represent you?

DEFENDANT   You don't have to appoint a very good
lawyer, I'm going to plead guilty.

. . . .

The defendant was in custody. At
arraignment he insisted that a mistake had
been made and that he was not the person
the judge thought he was. He refused to
admit he was the person charged, and
then asked what "that person" was
charged with committing.

THE COURT   Well, there are two cases. The first one is
minor—drunk in public—and if you plead
guilty I would give you credit for time
served and that case would be over. The

second case—battery—is more serious and
you should have a lawyer.

DEFENDANT O.K., I'll be that guy on the first case.

· · · · · · · · · · · · · · ·

While working his criminal calendar,
the judge called the case of *People v.
Steven Lewon Crook.* The bailiff opened
the door to the holding cell and called
"Crook, come forward." Five prisoners
walked from the cell into the courtroom!

· · · · · · · · · · · · · · ·

The defendant, charged with arson,
missed a court appearance.

THE COURT Where were you?
DEFENDANT In the hospital.
THE COURT Why?
DEFENDANT Smoke inhalation.

· · · · · · · · · · · · · · ·

DEFENSE COUNSEL Are you sure you did not enter the
Seven-Eleven on 40th and N.E. Broadway
and hold up the cashier on June 17 of this
year?

DEFENDANT I'm pretty sure.

8

WITNESSES

"*Wherefore seeing we also are compassed about with so great a cloud of witnesses . . . , let us run with patience the race that is set before us.*"

HEBREWS, 12:1–2

"*Then call them to our presence; face to face; and frowning brow to brow, ourselves will hear the accuser and the accused freely speak.*"
WILLIAM SHAKESPEARE, RICHARD II

"*They cudden't get me into coort as a witness; no, sir, not if't was to hang me best friend. 'T is hard enough with newspapers an' cinsus officers an' th' mim'ry iv cab dhrivers to live down ye'er past without bein' foorced to dhrill it in a r-red coat an' with a brass band ahead befure th' eyes iv th' multitood. I did it wanst; I'll do it no more.*"
MR. DOOLEY (FINLEY PETER DUNNE)

COUNSEL   (examining a witness with eyesight
          problems) How many fingers am I holding
          up?
THE COURT The record will show the attorney is
          holding up two fingers.

. . . .

COUNSEL   Do you have any sort of medical disability?
WITNESS   Legally blind.
COUNSEL   Does that create substantial problems with
          your eyesight as far as seeing things?

. . . .

PROSECUTOR All right. Do you feel that you got a good
           look at the face of the person who had
           pointed that gun at your face initially and
           took you into the laundry room?
WITNESS   Yes, sir, I do.
PROSECUTOR If I asked you to look around the
           courtroom now, do you see the person who
           pointed that gun at you? If you would like
           to stand up, you may.
WITNESS   Yes, sir.
PROSECUTOR You do? Could you please indicate for us
           where he is located and what he is wearing
           so we all know who you are talking about?
WITNESS   The gentleman seated at the desk over
           there.
PROSECUTOR Okay, I have no further questions.
THE COURT Seated at what desk over there?

80

WITNESS	The desk against the wall.
DEFENSE COUNSEL	Your Honor, could the record indicate that the witness has identified the bailiff in the courtroom, who is a deputy sheriff?
THE COURT	He said you identified the deputy sheriff.
WITNESS	I did?
THE COURT	Yeah.
PROSECUTOR	Your Honor, I ask that that man be placed under arrest.
WITNESS	Well, I am sorry. I was going by what I thought I remembered.
THE COURT	I have never had that happen before. That is the first.
WITNESS	Oh, my glasses.
THE COURT	Oh. Can you see better without your glasses?
WITNESS	Yes, Your Honor. The color of the gentleman is the same.

. . . .

WITNESS	The person in the middle is not the one that was—he did not have the gun.
THE COURT	All right, ma'am. But that isn't the question. Let's do it this way. Are you sure that the person without the gun isn't the man on the left?
WITNESS	Yes. I'm sure he is not the one that had the gun.
THE COURT	Oh, no, the one without the gun. Are you sure it's not the person on the left?
WITNESS	Yes, I'm sure.
THE COURT	That he's not?

WITNESS	He's not the one without the gun.
THE COURT	Are you sure that the one in the middle is the one without the gun?
WITNESS	That's right. I'm sure he's not the one without the gun.
COUNSEL	Perhaps the Court could just ask if she recognizes him.

. . . .

COUNSEL	Calling your attention now to the defendant in the blue shirt, seated at the end of the counsel table, do you know him?
WITNESS	I have never seen the jerk before.
THE COURT	All right. Thank you very much, sir. You are excused. You may go.
WITNESS	I am excused, Your Honor?
THE COURT	You may go.
WITNESS	(to defendant) I better never see your butt in my place again ever.
THE COURT	All right, sir. That is enough.
WITNESS	Ever.

. . . .

COUNSEL	Did you give a description of the shirt?
WITNESS	Yes, I did.
COUNSEL	What color was the shirt?
WITNESS	It was a plaid shirt, and I told the deputy it had red, possibly some green or blue in the shirt, but it was plaid.
COUNSEL	How would you describe it? A dress shirt,

sort of like the one we're wearing, you're wearing, I'm wearing, or something different?

WITNESS   I'd describe it as the same shirt that individual [the defendant] is wearing right over there today.

. . . .

THE COURT   All right. Miss, after testifying here and thinking about it, would you take another look at this man seated here with defense counsel?

DEFENSE COUNSEL   Does she need to get closer? I don't have any objection.

WITNESS   No, this is fine.

THE COURT   You can recognize him all right? You can see him from where you are seated?

WITNESS   Yes.

PROSECUTOR   Do you want my glasses?

WITNESS   Yes, maybe I will—

THE COURT   No. I'd just as soon she don't have any glasses. Would you like to get about as close as you were?

WITNESS   Your Honor, he had more facial hair on him.

THE COURT   Do you think this is the same person or not?

WITNESS   If he had that white hat on I would be able to tell more, because I can't tell with the receding hairline and—it's hard to tell.

THE COURT   Do you think he is? Do you think he isn't? Do you know?

"I'm sorry, but counsel *must* take the witness."

WITNESS	He had the same face features, like I said earlier. The guy, to me, looked like a street guy.
DEFENSE COUNSEL	A what?
WITNESS	Somebody who looks on, like, "Laverne and Shirley." They got those two guys on "Laverne and Shirley." That guy that night looked a lot like one of them.
THE COURT	Squiggy or Lennie?

. . . .

DEFENSE COUNSEL	Now, you wear glasses, don't you?
WITNESS	No.
DEFENSE COUNSEL	You don't wear glasses?
WITNESS	No.
DEFENSE COUNSEL	You didn't have glasses on at the lineup?
WITNESS	Yes, I did. I don't wear them as a necessity to see. I just wear them to distinctify my vision a little bit better.

. . . .

CLERK	Please raise your right hand. You do solemnly swear that the testimony you may give in the cause now pending before this court shall be the truth, the whole truth, and nothing but the the truth, so help you God.
WITNESS	No. I don't because I don't even know why I'm here, what I'm here for or nothing. Period. I have no idea why I'm here.

85

THE COURT	You have been brought in as a witness.
WITNESS	Witness for who?
THE COURT	Brought in as a witness by the district attorney's office.
WITNESS	A witness for the district attorney's office? That's a damn lie. By whose orders? I'd like to know what the hell is going on. I have did nothing. I haven't talked to nobody. I don't know anything what's been happening.
THE COURT	There are no charges against you.
WITNESS	I don't care if there is charges against me. I wouldn't be for the district attorney's office if there were charges against me. Period.
THE COURT	You were brought in as a witness.
WITNESS	Why? From who? Who said what? Who did what? Ain't nobody told me nothing about this shit.
THE COURT	You haven't been asked any any questions.
WITNESS	I'm not going to answer any questions.
THE COURT	You haven't been asked any questions.
WITNESS	I'm not going to answer any questions because I don't know a Goddamn thing. I don't even know why I'm here. I sure like an explanation. They take me out of Folsom with a broken leg Saturday. I ain't got it fixed yet or a cast on it. Hell, no. And regardless, I'm going to tell you out front I have been down over fourteen years and I wouldn't testify for my mother if she was on trial for no district attorney.

86

	That's final. Period. Let me out of here. Don't try this shit no more.
THE COURT	Are you going to refuse to be sworn as a witness?
WITNESS	I'm refusing everything. I don't even know who's on trial here. Me? For what? I ain't did nothing.
THE COURT	You're not on trial here. You were brought in—
WITNESS	Who's on trial here?
D.A.	Your Honor, I wonder perhaps if the witness might have counsel appointed to represent him?
WITNESS	Don't give me no counsel. I don't want no counsel.
D.A.	To advise him as to the nature of the proceedings and why he's here to testify.
WITNESS	I don't give a fuck why I'm here. Period. I wouldn't help your office. You just go ahead and kill me, brother, because I don't care. I have been a victim for fourteen years. Don't pull this shit with me. What the hell is wrong with the people down here? Who is going to trial here from the gate?
THE COURT	You can take him back into the lockup. The Court will appoint an attorney to talk to him.
WITNESS	(addressing the defendant) Are you going to trial, brother?
DEFENDANT	Yes.

WITNESS   What's you name?
DEFENDANT (omitted)
WITNESS   (still addressing the defendant) What the
           hell is wrong with these people right here?
           Big Ike says hello.

9

LEADING QUESTIONS

"The penalty for laughing in a courtroom is six months; if it were not for this penalty the jury would never hear the evidence."

H. L. MENCKEN

"If you can think about something that is related to something else without thinking about the thing to which it is related, then you have the legal mind."

THOMAS REED POWELL

"All interrogatories must, to some extent, make a suggestion to a witness. It would be perfectly nugatory to ask a witness, if he knew anything about something."

LORD LANGDALE

COUNSEL	Did you see any feces on the ground?
WITNESS	I didn't see any—I didn't see any fishes.
COUNSEL	Not fishes, feces.
WITNESS	Little frogs. No I didn't see any.
COUNSEL	When you don't pass water, when you do number two.
WITNESS	What do you mean?
COUNSEL	In other words, did he pass food through his body?
WITNESS	I don't understand.
COUNSEL	Okay. Pardon me ladies and gentlemen. Did he take a shit? Did you see any of that?
WITNESS	I didn't see that, no.
COUNSEL	Did you smell it?
WITNESS	Why should I go and smell his shit?

· · · · · · · · · · · · · · · ·

THE COURT	I thought the six-foot fence was to the south?
WITNESS	Well the West Side is kind of confusing. Normally a person would say that north and south runs east and west if you were north of the tracks. And some persons say they would be east and west if you were south of the tracks. So I use north and south. And that's—the report the detective has is opposite. But the way the report has—the way the detective has it in the report, he would have been rolled south, which would have been east, if you can understand what I'm saying.

90

. . . .

COUNSEL   All right. Was there some event, Valerie, that occurred which kind of finally made you determine that you had to separate from your husband?

WITNESS   Yes.

COUNSEL   Did he try to do something to you?

WITNESS   Yes.

COUNSEL   What did he do?

WITNESS   Well, uh, he tried to kill me.

COUNSEL   All right. And then you felt that that was the last straw; is that correct?

WITNESS   Right.

. . . .

COUNSEL   Is Jerry a man or woman?

WITNESS   A man.

COUNSEL   Do you know where he lives?

WITNESS   No, I do not.

COUNSEL   Do you know his telephone number?

WITNESS   No, I do not. I think Judy do.

COUNSEL   Can you describe him for us?

WITNESS   No, I—I don't know what he looks like. Black.

COUNSEL   He is black?

WITNESS   He is about 6 feet; short afro; has a mustache. I believe him and Judy has a relationship.

COUNSEL   What kind of relationship?

WITNESS   I think they fuck every now and then.

91

. . . .

WITNESS   He was saying he hated Anna and she was a dirty so and so and all this cussing and crap. I started telling him, you know, look, I don't like the cussing and all the stuff.

COUNSEL   Does that irritate you, him swearing?

WITNESS   Yes, it does.

COUNSEL   What'd he do next?

WITNESS   With both hands, drug me over to the bed, threw me around and kept choking the shit out of me.

. . . .

COUNSEL   Now, in the past you have received numerous threats from the defendant, haven't you?

WITNESS   Yes.

COUNSEL   And those threats were against—he was threatening your life?

WITNESS   Not my life. No, he just threatened to throw battery acid in my face.

. . . .

THE COURT   I got the *Quadrafini*, but then he said somebody played in it, and I didn't get that.

PROSECUTOR   The Who.

THE COURT   The what?

WITNESS   Musicians.

92

PROSECUTOR   The Who.

WITNESS   The Who.

THE COURT   Who?

WITNESS   The Who. That's the name of the band.

THE COURT   So that's the name of the group, The Who?

WITNESS   Yes, The Who.

THE COURT   Not The What? The Who?

WITNESS   No, The Who.

THE COURT   You got it, everybody? The *Quadrafini* is a movie with The Who.

WITNESS   Punk rockers.

THE COURT   All right.

. . . .

THE COURT   Would you lift it so I can describe it for the record?

The sergeant is pointing to an area, oh, I would say about two or three inches above his left wrist.

He is holding his left arm extended outward so the left side of his arm and hand are facing me, and it would be just at the spot where the front of the arm becomes the right side and back of the arm.

Is that clear enough for everybody?

. . . .

COUNSEL   I'd be glad to make an offer of proof with regard to that question about the tattoo

on her breast, but I think it should be
made.

THE COURT   The witness, by the way, for the record,
just asked me if I'd like to see it; and I
said, "No."

WITNESS   I mean, because it's not on my breast. It's
right on my chest.

COUNSEL   May the record reflect that she just
showed it to everybody in the court?

THE COURT   There it is.

WITNESS   Right there.

THE COURT   Some people call that a breast.

. . . .

D.A.   Have you come into court and lied against
Jessie?

WITNESS   No.

D.A.   Have you come to court and lied for
Philip?

WITNESS   No.

D.A.   Has anyone told you what to say here in
court?

WITNESS   No.

D.A.   Did any police officers tell you what to say
here in court?

WITNESS   No.

D.A.   Did Detective C. tell you what to say here
in court?

WITNESS   No.

D.A.   What did I tell you to say here in court?

WITNESS   (pause) Stick with the story.

. . . .

COUNSEL   Were you leaning up against the shut door
           or open door?
WITNESS   A shut door. How can you lean against an
           open door? There's a hole there. You'd fall
           through the hole.

. . . .

COUNSEL   Do you think that based upon these
           observations that you stated that you had,
           and conversations with neighbors, have you
           been able to form an opinion as to
           whether she is a chaste or unchaste
           person?
WITNESS   Yes.
COUNSEL   And what is your opinion?
WITNESS   She is chased and she doesn't chase.
           When you go out and flag a guy down—I
           mean, you can't help it.
THE COURT Rephrase the question. Apparently the
           witness doesn't understand.
COUNSEL   Do you know—perhaps I'm not speaking
           clearly. Do you know the meaning of the
           word "chaste"?
WITNESS   No, I'm not sure what you mean.
COUNSEL   All right. The word "morality,"
           moral-morality versus immorality?
WITNESS   I don't believe she has any morals.

. . . .

"Objection, Your Honor. Counsel is leading the witness."

ᴅᴇFENSE COUNSEL	At any time did you hear any shots being fired?
WITNESS	Yes.
ᴅᴇFENSE COUNSEL	How many did you hear?
WITNESS	Two at first.
ᴅᴇFENSE COUNSEL	Okay. And could you tell us how fast those two shots were fired?
WITNESS	Like estimate you mean?
ᴅᴇFENSE COUNSEL	Yes.
WITNESS	Like bang, bang.
ᴅᴇFENSE COUNSEL	Okay. Now you recall testifying at the preliminary hearing, correct?
WITNESS	Correct.
ᴅᴇFENSE COUNSEL	Okay. And at that time do you remember saying that the shots went, as opposed to bang, bang, the shots went bang bang?
WITNESS	What do you mean bang bang?
ᴅᴇFENSE COUNSEL	Well there is a difference, right, between bang, bang and bang bang?
WITNESS	I said, well I said bang, boom boom is what I said, right?
ᴅᴇFENSE COUNSEL	Okay. Is that correct, boom boom?
WITNESS	Yes.
ᴅᴇFENSE COUNSEL	Okay. And is that the way now that you recall the shots being fired, boom boom?
WITNESS	Boom boom. Well, really, the way it is like cap-gun like I said, like more of like a pop. I was saying like boom boom as an example.
ᴅᴇFENSE COUNSEL	Now can you describe, using whatever words you want, pop, boom, bang,

97

whatever, how fast you heard those shots go off?

WITNESS   Boom, boom.

. . . .

PLAINTIFF'S COUNSEL   What doctor treated you for the injuries you sustained while at work?

WITNESS   Dr. J.

PLAINTIFF'S COUNSEL   And what kind of physician is Dr. J.?

WITNESS   Well, I'm not sure, but I remember that you said he was a good plaintiff's doctor!

. . . .

COUNSEL   Could you briefly describe the type of construction equipment used in your business?

WITNESS   Four tractors.

COUNSEL   What kind of tractors are they?

WITNESS   Fords.

COUNSEL   Did you say "four?"

WITNESS   Ford. Ford. Like the Ford. It is a Ford tractor.

COUNSEL   You didn't say "four," you just said "Ford?"

WITNESS   Yes, Ford. That is what you asked me, what kind of tractors.

COUNSEL   Are there four Ford tractors? Is that what it is?

WITNESS   No, no. You asked me what kind of a tractor it was and I said Ford tractors.

COUNSEL   How many tractors are there?

WITNESS   Four.

. . . .

FENSE COUNSEL   The truth of the matter is that you are not an unbiased, objective witness, isn't it? You, too were shot in the fracas?

WITNESS   No, sir. I was shot midway between the fracas and the naval.

. . . .

The defendant herein, having been first duly sworn, was examined and testified as follows:

THE COURT   Mr. Guzman, can you read and write and understand the English language?

DEFENDANT   Si.

10

CROSS EXAMINATION

"More cross-examinations are suicidal than homicidal."
                                    EMORY R. BUCKNER

"Whosoever diggeth a pit shall fall therein: and he that rolleth a stone, it will return upon him."
                                    PROVERBS, 26:27

WITNESS	You know what, I'm tired of this game. I got nothing to say.
D.A.	Did you become familiar, have you become familiar with the convict code?
WITNESS	I'm familiar with a lot of things.
D.A.	And you are familiar with the convict code, right?
WITNESS	I let you assume all that. Because that's all you're doing, your just blowing it out of your ass.
D.A.	Now, under the convict code is it allowed for one convict to testify for the prosecution against another convict?
WITNESS	You know how I will answer that? Two easy ways [holds up middle two fingers] subtract one [vulgar gesture].
D.A.	And as you sit there today, you have a very strong dislike for me, correct?
WITNESS	For you, your mother, your dog, your grandfather, everybody else about you.
D.A.	And the reason that you very strongly dislike me is because of the fact that you feel I'm placing your life in danger by calling you as a witness, right?
WITNESS	You want to know? Currently, I'm housed in Folsom Prison and by you calling me down here, you fuck me out of my handball games. I had a hundred dollars money game going. You going to compensate me for that?
D.A.	That's the only reason why you dislike me as the prosecutor, right?
WITNESS	I'm a capitalist at heart.

. . . .

EFENSE COUNSEL	Answer the question. When did they have a knife at your throat?
WITNESS	That was a figure of speech.
EFENSE COUNSEL	So they had a figure of speech at your throat?

. . . .

PROSECUTOR	You remember Good Friday, don't you? Do you remember what the previous Sunday, May 14th was? What date it was?
WITNESS	That Sunday before the 17th of May?
PROSECUTOR	Uh-huh.
WITNESS	I believe it was Mother's Day.
PROSECUTOR	Were you thinking of your mother when you committed that homicide?
EFENSE COUNSEL	Your Honor, I would object to that as argumentative.
PROSECUTOR	Or your mother-in-law?
THE COURT	Sustained.
PROSECUTOR	Do you remember what May 20th, 1978, it was the following Saturday?
WITNESS	May 20th I was in jail.
PROSECUTOR	You don't know what day it was? That was Armed Forces Day, wasn't it?
THE COURT	I wonder whether that is a material test of his recollection. I have flown in combat and I don't know when Armed Forces Day is, but maybe some people do. All right.

PROSECUTOR	But you remember what day Good Friday was? You had to come in and tell us that, what day Good Friday was?
WITNESS	Yes. I remember what day Good Friday was on.
PROSECUTOR	You know who gets condemned more than even liars and killers in the Scripture? Well, let me ask you, do you know what a hypocrite is?
DEFENSE COUNSEL	Once again, I would object to that.
THE COURT	Sustained, argumentative.

. . . .

PROSECUTOR	You pretty much hate the defendant though, don't you?
WITNESS	No, not really. I just think he is a crazy kid. That's all.
PROSECUTOR	Didn't you describe him before as a punk, liar, thief, cheat and murderer and the lowest form of life that you know?
WITNESS	Yeah. That pretty well sums him up. But he is a crazy kid on top of that.

. . . .

COUNSEL	Were you ever in the military service?
WITNESS	I was.
COUNSEL	And when were you in the military service?
WITNESS	World War II.
COUNSEL	And what years were they?

WITNESS   September 1939 until April 1945.
COUNSEL   And during that period of time was it not
             a fact that there was segregation in the
             Armed Forces?
D.A.   Your Honor, I'd object as irrelevant.
COUNSEL   Bias.
THE COURT   Segregation? On what grounds?
COUNSEL   Racial grounds.
WITNESS   Not to my knowledge.
COUNSEL   You are not aware that the Armed Forces
             —that Truman in 1944 ordered the
             desegregation of Armed Forces?
D.A.   I object as irrelevant.
THE COURT   The objection is sustained.
COUNSEL   I think the court can take judicial notice
             the Armed Forces were segregated by race
             until Truman ordered them desegregated
             as President of the United States.
WITNESS   I was in the Canadian Army.

. . . .

COUNSEL   Do you know whether they were 45
             records or those big ones?
WITNESS   Yes, 45.
COUNSEL   They were little 45 records?
WITNESS   Yes.
COUNSEL   Do you remember what the song was,
             Mabel?
WITNESS   "Things I Used To Do I Won't Do No
             More."
COUNSEL   "Things I Used To Do I Won't Do No
             More?"

"All right, you two! Break it up!"

WITNESS That's that record. You ask George [the defendant] there. I play that all time. Can I talk to him? Is that right, George? That's what I play, ain't it?

THE COURT Wait a minute. You can't talk to the defendant.

WITNESS Well, I asked him could I.

THE COURT You'll have to ask me. I run this here business.

WITNESS Oh, well, I'm sorry. I didn't think you knowed the record; you wasn't up there.

THE COURT The only record I know is, "What Lilbert [the deceased] used to know, Lilbert don't know no more."

WITNESS Yeah, he's played his last one.

. . . .

D.A. Mr. C., you testified on your direct examination that quote it takes a lots to make me angry. Close quote. Is that true?

WITNESS Yes, because I don't like to get angry. I feel I can resolve problems without getting angry. The only time I may be offensive is if someone attack me.

D.A. You figure you're a basically peaceful person?

WITNESS I tries to be.

D.A. Your wife is named Willetta, is that correct?

WITNESS Yes.

D.A. On December the 19th, 1981, did you hit Willetta in the face with a two-by-four?

WITNESS It was not a two-by-four. It was a one-by-three.

11

EXPERT WITNESSES

"I am firmly of the belief that jurors are quite capable of seeing through flaky testimony and pseudo-scientific clap-trap. I quite agree that we should not waste our valuable court time watching witch doctors, voo-doo practitioners, or brujas go through the entrails of dead chickens in a fruitless search for the truth."
JUSTICE ROBERT A. GARDNER

"Expert opinion is only an ordinary guess in evening clothes."
JUSTICE CURTIS BOK

"There are three kinds of witnesses: liars, damned liars, and experts."
ANONYMOUS

COUNSEL	And you are involved I take it in both aspects of pathology here in your practice?
WITNESS	Yes. I am certified in both.
COUNSEL	Directing your attention to the 6th of November 1976, in the evening hours, do you recall being up at Rose Chapel in Paradise?
WITNESS	Yes.
COUNSEL	Do you recall examining a person by the name of Rodney Edgington at the funeral chapel?
WITNESS	Yes.
COUNSEL	Do you recall approximately the time that you examined the body of Mr. Edgington at the Rose Chapel?
WITNESS	It was in the evening. The autopsy started at about 8:30 P.M.
COUNSEL	And Mr. Edginton was dead at that time, is that correct?
WITNESS	No, you dumb asshole. He was sitting on the table wondering why I was doing an autopsy.

. . . .

DEFENSE COUNSEL	Are there some types of rules or a code of ethics among prostitutes and their employer?
D.A.	Objection. It calls for an expert opinion. It's also vague as to time and place.
THE COURT	Foundation, counsel. I don't believe there is any foundation for this.

110

D.A.	May I take the witness on *voir dire?*
THE COURT	Yes.
D.A.	Mr. P, pimps don't have organizations like other professions have, do they?
WITNESS	They are organized.
D.A.	Are there conventions where pimps get together and discuss mutual problems and things of that nature?
WITNESS	They have what you would call pimp conventions.
D.A.	Mr. P., do you consider yourself to be a student of pimpology or the study of pimping?
WITNESS	Well, I have hung around a lot of them.
D.A.	Any particular reason why?
WITNESS	Because I wanted to know about it. I wanted to know the different backgrounds, the ways that they ran their system and the motions, the steps, because I wanted to make mine different.

. . . .

D.A.	What is the meaning of sperm being present?
WITNESS	It indicates intercourse.
D.A.	Male sperm?
WITNESS	That is the only kind I know.

. . . .

COUNSEL	Doctor, would you be surprised if you saw the defendant talking to himself?

111

WITNESS   Not in the least.

COUNSEL   Why is that?

WITNESS   He doesn't have any friends.

. . . .

PROSECUTOR   Would you briefly describe your background with respect to bullets and ammunition?

DEFENSE COUNSEL   I am going to object to this, Your Honor, unless the district attorney can make an offer of proof that this man is an expert, and I don't want to hear that he has been shooting bullets since he was ten.

THE COURT   It will be overruled.

WITNESS   I have been interested in shooting basically since I was ten years old, both cartridge-type ammunition and also black power. I do my own reloading for my guns. I have a reloading press at home and powder and all that stuff.

PROSECUTOR   What is your background with respect to .22 ammunition?

WITNESS   I have purchased a lot of it.

. . . .

COUNSEL   The respiratory arrest means no breathing, doesn't it?

WITNESS   That's right.

COUNSEL   And in every case where there is a death, isn't there no breathing?

. . . .

FENSE ATTORNEY	How would you expect somebody to react being stabbed six times in this fashion?
WITNESS	At one point as he is being stabbed he is going to hurt.
FENSE ATTORNEY	And would that be debilitating in any way, limit somebody's ability to move around or to function in any way?
WITNESS	It might slow him down a little.

. . . .

COUNSEL	OK. Now, let's translate that, doctor. Reddish discoloration is a more recent sort of injury; is that correct?
WITNESS	More fresh.
COUNSEL	Fresh?
WITNESS	More fresh.
COUNSEL	More fresh.
WITNESS	Not fresh fresh, but more fresh than recent.

. . . .

COUNSEL	Now, you also testified that you tried to run a test that the matter was cocaine, is that right?
POLICE OFFICER	I tried to run a water test on it.
COUNSEL	What did the test consist of?
POLICE OFFICER	The substance looked something like soap powder, so we ran water in the portable

113

bar that was in the room and the sergeant tried to see what would happen to the cocaine as the water hit it.

COUNSEL   What was supposed to have happened?

POLICE OFFICER   If it was cocaine it would have immediately have dissolved.

COUNSEL   What would have happened if that was soap?

POLICE OFFICER   It would have dissolved.

. . . .

COUNSEL   Are you qualified to give a urine sample?

WITNESS   Yes, I have been since early childhood.

. . . .

DEFENSE COUNSEL   So if I hit the prosecutor at this very moment and he fell over the back of this railing, hit his head and a subdural hematoma immediately began to form, the blood that was leaking into the space would have essentially the same components as the blood leaking into his teeny little brain?

. . . .

THE COURT   In this case the request is made for the appointment of the psychologist for the performance of an IQ test. The court does not see the need for an IQ test since it appears to me that he is dumber than a fencepost.

COUNSEL Has the court stated it in numerical terms?

THE COURT His IQ is less than zero.

. . . .

COUNSEL What device do you have in your laboratory to test alcohol content?

WITNESS I have a dual column gas chromatograph, Hewlett-Packard 5710A with flame analyzation detectors.

THE COURT Can you get that with mag wheels?

WITNESS Only on the floor models.

. . . .

COUNSEL Could you describe your duties as a forensic analyst?

WITNESS I analyze narcotics; I analyze blood, breath and urine samples for alcohol, I analyze blood and urine samples for drugs. I analyze all types of physical evidence for blood, and I do sex fiend cases, assault cases, homicide cases, anything like that.

. . . .

COUNSEL Let me rephrase it. It was kind of poorly phrased.

THE COURT Most of your questions are, but that's okay. Want to start over?

"May I ask you to call for quiet, Your Honor? My witness is about to share his expertise."

COUNSEL If you had estimated the fetal weight as of August 15, 1978, do you have any opinion as to what your estimate would have been?

WITNESS I think that's impossible. I don't any—I—I don't think I could answer it, because I don't think I know.

You're asking me to guess what I would have guessed if I had tried to guess, and I didn't try to guess; so I don't know what I would have tried to guess or what I would have guessed.

· · · · · · · · · · · · · · ·

Argument heading in an appellant's opening brief:

THE TRIAL COURT ERRED IN ORDERING A MEDICAL EXAMINATION OF APPELLANT'S PENIS IN HIS ABSENCE.

· · · · · · · · · · · · · · ·

COUNSEL Now, in your report under "Foundation" you indicated there is a minimum of cracking and no signs of settling.

WITNESS Yes.

COUNSEL When you say there is a minimum of cracking, I take it that you did find some cracking.

WITNESS No. Because if I said there was no

cracking, I would be in court just like this answering some stupid lawyers' questions. So I put minimum in there to cover myself, because somebody is going to find a crack somewhere.

THE COURT I could say I would like to shake your hand, but I won't.

COUNSEL Move to strike—

THE COURT No. We are not going to strike it.

COUNSEL Move to strike the word "stupid," Your Honor.

THE COURT The most appropriate word you want stricken? It is worth the whole trial.

. . . .

The following ad was placed in the Los Angeles *Daily Journal* on April 8, 1980:

Alienist Wanted
"Alphabet Bomber," Chief Military Officer of "Aliens of America," acting in propria persona, is seeking the assistance of an alienist, capable of advanced intellectual gymnastics, (yet free of the side effects of intellectual hallucinogens and ideological brain damage), and interested in defining a scientific formula of the relationship of intellectual and mental competence within the meaning of 1368 PC and as applied to a condition where a defendant in a mass murder trial

118

believes to be The Messiah, and has set
up his own arrest due to his "delusion"
that he must prove in the court of law of
the "City of Angels" that he is The
Messiah, and thus establish the legality of
his world rulership.

This project presupposes one's ability
to temporarily case away all socio-religious
illusions and traditions and base one's
thinking entirely on cold facts in total
absence of emotion, and this project shall
be illuminated by the presumption of
innocence; by the classic example of the
difference between sane and insane;
(2,000 years ago a man who believed that
earth is round was insane and today a
man who believes that earth is flat is
insane); by the scientific truths that there
is an exception to every rule; and by the
historical truths that the might defines
the right.

This project is neither an opportunity
for a $50 an hour license owning babelist,
nor a $100 an hour cloud-riding
conclusionist, but an opportunity for a
young, unbrainwashed, tradition
uninhibited, ideology immune, methodic
scientist.

12

CREATIVE DEFENSES

"Justice is not to be taken by storm. She is to be wooed by slow advances."

JUSTICE BENJAMIN N. CARDOZO

"I will look, Your Honor, and endeavor to find a precedent, if you require it; though it would seem to be a pity that the Court should lose the honor of being the first to establish so just a rule."

RUFUS CHOATE

DEFENDANT   What records I had, I had in my garage. I got a Labrador dog that floats over a seven-foot fence like an airplane. He is on probation, and if he bites one more person we are going to put him to sleep. For the last two years, he's been kept in my garage. He ate up a couch, so I mean the records where I have them stacked on this table, he completely ate them all, and some we are able to save, and we are in the process, which I told my attorney, and I have been spending a lot of time in trying to get these records straight.

COUNSEL   What records are those? This is the first we have heard about this. We have asked you questions about records. This is the first time we hear the dog defense.

· · · · · · · · · · · · · · · ·

OFFER OF PROOF   It was defendant's position that due to his limited education, background and experience, and his alleged cultural deficiencies, he lacked the wherewithal to perpetrate the evasion of his federal income tax. To this end, defendant intended to call Dr. Bruce to testify as to his findings with respect to defendant's intellectual capacity based upon certain tests and examinations conducted by him on the defendant. His defense was simply that he was too stupid willfully to violate

122

the Internal Revenue Code and that the expert would testify as to the defendant's stupidity.

THE COURT   In this matter, the Court is, of course, aware of the explanation given by the defendant for his reason for having this particular weapon in his possession at the time the search was made of his home. And, as I recall, he stated that he had possession of the weapon in order to change the holster for the weapon from a right-handed to left-handed holster, which he proposed to do by reversing it or turning the holster inside out. An examination of the holster would indicate that that proposal was ridiculous and I think the jury found the explanation equally ridiculous and convicted him of the charge.

COUNSEL   Your Honor, you heard the matter without a jury.

THE COURT   I did?

COUNSEL   Yes.

THE COURT   Then I found it ridiculous.

. . . .

FENSE COUNSEL   I am prepared to go to trial on this case. Now, my investigator fully investigated this case. I have talked to the defendant several times; he advises me that before we go to trial certain things must be done.

Number one, he wants to have a professional makeup man get him up in several different disguises.

. . . .

THE COURT	How do you plead at this time, guilty or not guilty of the charges?
DEFENDANT	Not guilty by reason of total love.
COUNSEL	Your Honor, I would indicate first that when I spoke with him today he had indicated that he wished to proceed pro per representing himself.
DEFENDANT	That is right, Your Honor.
THE COURT	Why is that?
DEFENDANT	Because I am the only one that can try this case properly, and I am very well talented. I have fifteen years studying canon law.
THE COURT	Which kind of law?
DEFENDANT	Canon law that all laws are based on. The laws of God apply to all cases. Canon law is the law of Moses, is that not right? And the Ten Commandments are the law of Moses. All laws are based on the Ten Commandments; so they have to derive and come from them, right?
THE COURT	No, no, no. I am not going to allow you to represent yourself at this point.
DEFENDANT	I have already passed the psychiatric examinations, three of them. Dr. Morgan has given me a total far out. Dr. Morgan

is a Christian. He believes like I do.

THE COURT He's given you a total far out, is that what you said?

DEFENDANT As a matter of fact, Your Honor, he said if Jesus Christ was in jail He'd be sitting with me in my same cell. Do I need any more?

. . . .

COUNSEL Yes. Has Mollie Frickle [the deceased] ever threatened you in any manner?

WITNESS Yes.

COUNSEL On more than one occasion?

WITNESS Yes.

COUNSEL Would you describe any injuries that you have suffered at her hands.

WITNESS On numerous occasions she's taken out a knife and threw it at me. But, the only injury I can truthfully say I ever suffered is when she grabbed me by the ear, you know, and with a knife, just—what can I say? Tore my ear. I guess that's the only thing, she tore my ear. She scratched it like this and tore my ear.

COUNSEL Did your ear bleed as a result of that?

WITNESS Only for four weeks.

COUNSEL Did she ever make any verbal threats to you as to what she would do to you?

WITNESS Yes.

COUNSEL What did she say in that regard?

WITNESS She said she was going to cut my balls off.

"In extenuation, Your Honor, may I point out that my
client cannot read English?"

. . . [S]he threatened me, the time she threatened Mike, the time she threatened Herman, my son, my cousin, her brother. She was a vile old lady. On numerous occasions, more than once and less than a thousand, but on numerous occasions she told Mike that his girl friend was a triple cunted whore. I am not sure what that means. I assume that it means that—

COUNSEL   Sir, do you recall anything that—anything in particular that Mollie Frickle said she would do to the defendant?

WITNESS   Yes.

COUNSEL   Can you tell us what that was?

WITNESS   I—on one occasion she said she was going to cut his balls off, and this is the way Mollie Frickle talked, and put them in a washing machine and just flush them like down to Long Beach.

COUNSEL   How old was Mollie Frickle at the time of her death, if you know?

WITNESS   Seventy-seven, seventy-two, I guess.

. . . .

COUNSEL   And what happened after you had been listening to the music for awhile?

WITNESS   We got held up.

COUNSEL   And what happened? Would you give the judge the details of that?

WITNESS   Well, they told us to get up against the wall, throw our money on the floor, and drop our pants.

127

COUNSEL   And what did you do?

WITNESS   Got against the wall, threw my pants
down, and threw our money down.

COUNSEL   I mean after you got up against the wall
and went through—or followed his
directions, what happened?

WITNESS   Cracked up laughing, because one of the
other guys—guys in on it dropped his
pants, too.

COUNSEL   Excuse me. One of the robbers?

WITNESS   Right.

COUNSEL   He took off his pants, also?

WITNESS   Right.

COUNSEL   And what happened as he did that?

WITNESS   They told him, "Not you stupid." And he
picked up the money.

13

CLOSING ARGUMENT

"Wisdom too often never comes, and so one ought not to reject it merely because it comes late."

JUSTICE FELIX FRANKFURTER

"He can compress the most words into the smallest idea of any man I ever met."

ABRAHAM LINCOLN

A criminal defense lawyer is making his closing argument to the jury. His client is accused of murder, but the body of the victim has never been found. He dramatically withdraws his pocket watch and announces to the jury, "Ladies and gentlemen, I have some astounding news. We have found the supposed victim of this murder alive and well, and, in exactly one minute, he will walk through that door into this courtroom."

A hushed silence falls over the courtroom, as everyone waits for the momentous entry. Nothing happens.

The lawyer then says, "The mere fact that you were watching that door, expecting the victim to walk into this courtroom, suggests that you have a reasonable doubt whether a murder was committed." Pleased with the impact of the stunt, he then sits down to await an acquittal.

The jury is instructed, files out and files back in 10 minutes later with a verdict finding the defendant guilty. Following the proceedings, the astounded lawyer chases after the jury foreman to find out what went wrong. "How could you convict?" he asks. "You were all watching the door!"

The foreman explains, "Most of us were watching the door. But one of us was watching the defendant, and he wasn't watching the door."

. . . .

EFENSE COUNSEL   I think one particular remark my client
was offended by that the D.A. made was
his exhortation to the jury to convict the
defendant in order to celebrate the
Bicentennial.

. . . .

PROSECUTOR   Now, my personal opinion as to whether
or not he's guilty, that doesn't mean a
thing, because I have not testified in this
case. But defense counsel gave his opinion,
and I'm going to give you mine. The
son-of-a-bitch (indicating) is guilty as hell.

D.A.   I told you I thought the defense counsel
was throwing out a lot of red herrings in
this case. About halfway through this trial
I believe that you sensed something
smelled funny here. Here's what that smell
is coming from (whereupon, the D.A.
presented the defense lawyer with a pile of
cow manure mounted on a plaque. A
motion for mistrial was denied.)

. . . .

Defense Argument To Jury In Prostitution
Case

> Now, you know, sex is as old as the
> world, ladies and gentlemen, and it will

131

be bought and sold whether you condemn it here or choose to look the other way. Well, for my client, this is a serious case. For the government, it is a serious case. But you know, for anyone with a little common sense, this case is an extravagant folly; cops flown in from Indiana, Minnesota, Missouri, Georgia, Michigan, FBI from Washington, handwriting expert, hotel detectives from Louisiana, a hotel detective who can't remember which room it was in, and his report can't help you straighten it out, motel records from all over, pounds of paper, movie screens, fancy projectors. A huge production. For what? Organized crime? No. Bank robbers? No. Hijackers? No. For what? For kids selling pussy.

D.A.'S Entire Closing Argument In A Drunk Driving Case

> *Roses are red*
> *Violets are blue*
> *Point one five*
> *means drunk to you.*

The verdict was guilty.

. . . .

D.A.   All you have to decide is whether based on the evidence that you've heard you're

satisfied beyond a reasonable doubt that
that's the man.

I read a story in *Reader's Digest* the
other day. Seems there were two attorneys.
And one attorney was married, and he had
a suspicion that when he would go out of
town to interview clients or make court
appearances in other cities, that his wife
was carrying on with a younger man.

So he got this friend of his, who was
available in the evening, and he said to his
friend, "Would you mind for the next
three days, while I'm gone, to sort of keep
an eye out on my wife and on our house
and see whether she has any visitors, and
let me know about it when I come back?"

So this second lawyer did that. And he
sort of hid in the weeds across the street
from the first lawyer's house. And, sure
enough, the following night, a car pulled
up, and a young man got out and went in
the house. And the lawyer sat there and
he watched all of this going on. And he
was taking notes on his legal pad, that all
lawyers carry with them at all times.

At the end of the evening when his
report was finished, he got on the phone
and he called the other attorney, the
attorney who lived in this house. And he
told the attorney, "I saw this car drive up;
I saw this young man get out; I saw him
go to the door, knock on it; a couple of

133

"But perhaps I digress."

minutes later, the door opened, and your wife opened the door and let him in."

And the attorney said, "Well, what happened then?" And the other guy said, "Well then I saw them go in the living room and they sat down; they talked for a little while, and then your wife got up, and she went into the kitchen. And she opened the refrigerator, pulled out a half gallon of wine, she poured a couple of glasses of wine, brought them into the living room and the two of them sat there and they drank the wine."

And the husband said, "What happened then?"

And the other lawyer said, "And then when they finished the wine, they got up, and she took his hand and then I saw them walk out of the living room and then they disappeared from my view."

And then the lawyer said, "Well, what happened then?" And the other lawyer said, "Well, then I saw the light come on upstairs, then I saw the two of them come into the bedroom, and I saw them embrace and kiss."

And the husband said, "Well, what happened then?" And the other lawyer said, "Well, your wife went over and turned out the light switch and I couldn't see anything that happened after that."

And the husband said, "Damn, that reasonable doubt."

I don't think I really have to expand on that story, ladies and gentlemen. There's no reasonable doubt in this case. There's a possible doubt. But there's no reasonable doubt.

14

JURY INSTRUCTIONS
AND DELIBERATIONS

"The naive assumption that prejudicial effects can be overcome by instructions to the jury . . . all practicing lawyers know to be unmitigated fiction."

JUSTICE ROBERT H. JACKSON

"Grand conglomerations of garbled verbiage and verbal garbage."

CHANNING POLLACK

JUROR   Your Honor, is it proper to ask the interpreter a question? I'm uncertain about the word la vado. You say that is a bar.

THE COURT   The court cannot permit jurors to ask questions directly. If you want to phrase your question to me—

JUROR   I understood it to be a restroom. I could better believe they would meet in a restroom rather than a public bar if he is undercover.

THE COURT   These are matters for you to consider. If you have any misunderstanding of what the witness testified to, tell the court now what you didn't understand and we'll place the—

JUROR   I understand the word la vado—I thought it meant restroom. She translates it as bar.

INTERPRETER   In the first place, the jurors are not to listen to the Spanish but to the English. I am a certified court interpreter.

JUROR   You're an idiot.

. . . .

Defendant's proposed instruction no. 7 assumption of risk:

> You are hereby instructed that when a person makes a decision to become a drug dealer he assumes the risk of: (1) being shot; (2) being killed; (3) being robbed; and (4) all of the above. 1 Rex 12 (1392).

138

Defendant's Proposed Instruction
No. 8:

> You are hereby instructed that any-
> body who kills four drug dealers can't be
> all bad.

· · · · · · · · · · · · · · ·

After the jury had been deliberating for
approximately six hours they came back into
the courtroom and asked for instructions on
premeditation, deliberation and specific intent.

THE COURT   I understand that you are confused by my
instructions on premeditation, deliteration
and Pacific intent. Those will now be read
back to you.

JURY FOREMAN   Your Honor, we would really just like to
take the written instructions back into the
jury room.

THE COURT   Okay, does counsel have any objections?

COUNSEL   No, Your Honor, but we would also like
them to have instructions on
preverification, deterioration and Atlantic
intent.

JURORS   [Laugh.]

D.A.   I think we should also throw in the Indian
Ocean Instruction.

THE COURT   Where have you guys been hiding out
during these deliberations?

COUNSEL   With you, Your Honor.

· · · · · · · · · · · · · · ·

The defendant challenged his conviction
on grounds the jury that tried him
conducted an unconstitutional experiment
to check key evidence in his case.

The woman he was convicted of raping
had testified she bit her assailant on the
arm during the attack, but could not
identify the defendant.

The prosecution relied on police
photographs of a bruise on one of the
defendant's arms when he was arrested
and on a doctor's testimony that the
bruise was caused by human teeth.

The defendant said he was bruised
when he scraped his arm on a chain-link
fence the night of the rape.

The jury, in trying to make up its mind,
conducted an experiment in which a
woman juror bit the foreman's arm.

The jurors then made periodic checks
on the resulting bruise and compared
it with the photos of the defendant's
arm.

. . . .

After three to four hours of deliberation
the jury indicated they were hung. The
judge asked them if further proceedings
could result in a verdict. The foreman
replied that they had taken a vote on
whether or not they were hung and that
vote was 6 to 6.

. . . .

The judge received the following note from the jury as they were deliberating a case:

"The jury stands at 10 to 2. One juror is obsessed with proof of intent. One juror sought guidance of prayer and was answered by God in her decision. Please instruct."

. . . .

The eight-man, four-woman jury had been deliberating for 20 hours when, at 5:30 P.M., it found itself still stuck at 9 to 3 in favor of conviction.

Within a few minutes, the judge received a note from the foreman: "Juror number 10 has locked herself in the girl's restroom. She has not responded to our notes. What shall we do?"

The juror refused to respond to other jurors when they talked to her from the other side of the restroom door. She remained holed up there for more than 15 minutes.

After receiving the foreman's note, the judge asked the other jurors to come back into the courtroom. Meanwhile, the bailiff successfully coaxed juror number 10 out of the restroom.

The judge declared a mistrial.

141

"We find the defense incompetent, the prosecution
arrogant, the food inedible, the accommodations
insufferable, and the defendant guilty as Hell."

. . . .

DEFENSE COUNSEL At this time I would request, since a motion is going to be held in this courtroom, a motion to suppress identification from the victim of a particular lineup, that the jury be excused from the jury room. I believe they can hear the testimony which will be presented in the courtroom.

THE COURT Let the record show that we are in a five million dollar courthouse, that this is the courtroom where the case has been assigned, that it's a brand new jury room, well insulated; that the jury is in the jury room and it is the opinion of the court that they can't hear anything that is going on because the jury is presently conversing and we can't hear them.

DEFENSE COUNSEL How do we know they are conversing?

THE COURT Can't you hear them?

. . . .

THE COURT Have you arrived at a verdict?

FOREMAN Yes, we have.

THE COURT Please give the verdicts to the bailiff. Please read them.

CLERK "We the jury impaneled to try the above-entitled cause find the defendant guilty."

JUROR Wait a minute!

CLERK | I am sorry, Your Honor. That's wrong. This isn't signed.

THE COURT | This isn't signed? What did you read it for? Start again.

Looks like you won't have your job very long after this, I can assure you.

CLERK | "We the jury impaneled to try the above-entitled cause find the defendant not guilty."

. . . .

The judge was finishing his oral charge to a jury. Being a judge who keeps up with the times, he pointed out in the verdict form where the "foreperson" should sign the verdict.

When the verdict was delivered later to the courtroom deputy, four persons had signed their names on the form.

He now uses the old-fashioned word "foreman."

15

SENTENCING

"My object all sublime,
I shall achieve in time,
To let the punishment fit the crime,
The punishment fit the crime."
      THE MIKADO
      (ARTHUR S. GILBERT)

THE COURT	I suppose the money found on the defendant at the time of his arrest came from this liquor store robbery.
DEFENDANT	No, that was bank robbery money.
THE COURT	Has anyone led you to believe the governor will pardon you if you plead guilty?
DEFENDANT	Well, I haven't been home, Judge, but he might have called my mother.

. . . .

The judge found himself locked outside his chambers along with the defendant and his defense attorney.

The defendant was about to be sentenced for a burglary conviction.

The judge called for a courthouse worker.

He tried keys, credit cards and a small drill, but failed to open the door.

"If you don't mind, Judge," said the defense lawyer, "I think my client can do this. He has a certain amount of expertise in this."

The judge approved. In three seconds his door was open. The judge thanked the defendant profusely.

"It was nothing at all, Judge, just professional courtesy," the defendant mumbled.

Minutes later, the judge sentenced him

146

to the maximum sentence—10 years in the state prison.

"If I need him again, I know where he will be," he said.

. . . .

An auto theft suspect who successfully applied for a bail reduction was returned to his cell, where he began yelling, cursing and making threats. His jailers hauled him back into court.

THE COURT   What's the problem?

DEFENDANT   [Profanities and insults.] If you ever want to tell me anything, mail it to me.

THE COURT   I won't have to mail you this—I'm finding you in contempt of court and sending you to county jail for one year.

DEFENDANT   Why not make it five years?

THE COURT   All right, you've got it.

DEFENDANT   Why not make it ten years?

THE COURT   You've got it—ten years in county jail.

DEFENDANT   Why not raise my bail to $50,000?

THE COURT   Bail will be set at $100,000.

. . . .

THE COURT   It is the judgment of this court that you be sentenced to the state prison at Deer Lodge for a term of ten years, the maximum penalty.

D.A.   Will that be dangerous or nondangerous offender, Your Honor?

THE COURT	Well, considering the flagrant nature of his offense, the court finds that he's a dangerous offender.
DEFENDANT	How in the hell can you find me a dangerous offender? There's nothing in there showing any violent crime. What's wrong with everybody anyway? You take that son-of-a-bitch and—
THE COURT	That will be it; you're remanded to the custody of the sheriff.
DEFENDANT	You son-of-a-bitch. You bald-headed son-of-a-bitch, when I get out of there, I'll blow your fucking head away. You no-good bald-headed son-of-a-bitch.
THE COURT	Get that down in the record, he's threatened to blow the judge's head off.
DEFENDANT	Stick it in your mouth you bald-headed bastard. You fucking son-of-a-bitch. You no-good bald-headed son-of-a-bitch.
THE COURT	If I could, I'd give you another ten years.

. . . .

. . . on a date to be hereafter fixed by order of this Court, within the State Prison, at which time and place you shall then and there put to death the said [defendant] in the manner prescribed by law. [But] . . . the Court finds you are entitled to credit for 549 days for time served and 182 days good time and work time, for a total of 731 days . . .

. . . .

THE COURT   All right. Any other questions?

DEFENDANT   How can you sentence an innocent man to prison?

THE COURT   It is part of my job.

. . . .

THE COURT   Is there anything else you would like to say before I pass sentence?

DEFENDANT   Yes, Kirk to Enterprise—Beam me up.

. . . .

Probation Report Excerpt

> The defendant gave the following brief story of his life:
> "I am youseley a home tipe of person you no tv music the you will think I all so lick cars going to the drive in is one of my things I hope that all thing come to an end at the drive in."
> *Education:*
> The defendant entered school in September 1965. He stated that the last school he attended was at San Diego City College. He stated he successfully completed his GED. The defendant appears to be of average intelligence and literacy.

. . . .

The defendant is an inveterate womanizer and a golf hustler. In short, he has no redeeming virtues.

. . . .

The undersigned officer has contacted the defendant's wife, but she will have nothing to do with him.

. . . .

Although somewhat large for his age, Tony appears somewhat smaller than he actually is.

. . . .

He indicated his marriage was happy, as he and his wife have always been sexually combatible.

. . . .

The boy was arrested for petty theft after the Earl Warren Junior High was broken in two.

. . . .

Defendant was seen loitering around a public restroom for the purpose of a lewd and lascivious act, namely the organ pavillion in the park.

. . . .

Defendant has been a crook all his life
and is still in the restaurant business.

. . . .

He was arrested for disturbing the
peach.

. . . .

This boy, a surfer, gets along well with
his pier group.

. . . .

The eldest and the youngest children
were gone, but the two middle-aged
children were still at home.

. . . .

Subject owes no one but the finance
company for his car and his mother.

. . . .

Defendant went to county hospital for
treatment of cut finger which he cut
accidentally while trying to cut wrist in
suicide attempt.

. . . .

"25 years! You call that revolving door justice?"

The defendant has made his own bed and now the probation officer feels that he should sleep in it.

. . . .

The man died, but he went to court and beat the case anyway.

. . . .

The defendant is charged with the theft of a roast from a meat market. The defendant acknowledged that before going to the market he pre-heated his oven.

. . . .

This twenty-three-and-a-half-year old defendant appears before the Court today for sentencing following alleged violations of his Superior Court probation grant on the convicted offense of robbery. He wishes this Court to believe that he has not lied to the probation officer and desires to remain on probation to "get a fresh start." If defendant received a nickel for every lie he has told, his net worth would rival the estate of the late Howard Hughes. His daily existence is so thoroughly interlaced with fabrication and deception that it is doubtful that he knows the truth. Whether he acquired the alias of "Watergate" from his unabated burglaries or from his use of Mr. Walter Gate's stolen business cards, remains to be seen. What is seen, as reported by the defendant's own mother and others, is that he has been terrorizing the west side of San Bernardino with his continual stealing.

To this officer, the most difficult problem in preparing this report was in finding the appropriate euphemisms needed to describe the character and behavior of defendant without risking a contempt of court charge. Suffice it to say that he is an abject pathological liar, a thief, and a plague upon the community. So long as he remains on the streets, he will represent a continued threat to the safety and property of innocent members of society. He is a true sociopath, showing no remorse for his actions and no regard whatsoever for the rights of other individuals.

In no way should he be reinstated on supervised probation. He has proven he does not have the capacity to function under supervision. All his psychic energy is used in creating lies for the probation officer, while all his physical energy is spent on stealing. Although the disposition appears too lenient for the crime of robbery, innocent members of the community will at least be spared defendant's foot through their front door for sixteen months.